AR: L W9-AJS-181

Harvest Time

by Jennifer Waters

Content and Reading Adviser: Joan Stewart
Educational Consultant/Literacy Specialist
New York Public Schools

Spyglass
BOOKS

COMPASS POINT BOOKS

Minneapolis, Minnesota

Compass Point Books
3722 West 50th Street, #115
Minneapolis, MN 55410

Visit Compass Point Books on the Internet at *www.compasspointbooks.com*
or e-mail your request to *custserv@compasspointbooks.com*

Photographs ©:
Richard Hamilton Smith, cover; PhotoDisc, 4, 5, 6; Visuals Unlimited/R. Calentine, 7; Two Coyote
Studios/Mary Walker Foley, 8; PhotoDisc, 9; Two Coyote Studios/Mary Walker Foley, 10; PhotoDisc, 11;
Two Coyote Studios/Mary Walker Foley, 12, 13, 14; Visuals Unlimited/John D. Cunningham, 15;
Two Coyote Studios/Mary Walker Foley, 16; PhotoDisc, 17, 18, 19; Two Coyote Studios/Mary
Walker Foley, 20, 21.

Project Manager: Rebecca Weber McEwen
Editor: Alison Auch
Photo Researcher: Jennifer Waters
Photo Selectors: Rebecca Weber McEwen and Jennifer Waters
Designer: Mary Walker Foley

Library of Congress Cataloging-in-Publication Data

Waters, Jennifer.
  Harvest time / by Jennifer Waters.
     p. cm. -- (Spyglass books)
Includes bibliographical references (p.   ).
Summary: Simple text and photographs describe how several different
crops, including pumpkins, corn, potatoes, and cranberries are picked
and gathered by humans and by machine.
  ISBN 0-7565-0239-X (hardcover)
  1. Food crops--Harvesting--Juvenile literature. 2.
Harvesting--Juvenile literature. [1. Food crops--Harvesting. 2.
Harvesting.] I. Title. II. Series.
  SB175 .W38 2002
  631.5'5--dc21
                              2001007324

© 2002 by Compass Point Books
All rights reserved. No part of this book may be reproduced without written permission from the publisher.
The publisher takes no responsibility for the use of any of the materials or methods described in this book,
nor for the products thereof.
Printed in the United States of America.

Contents

What Is a Harvest?

Harvest is the time
to pick and gather
ripe fruits and vegetables.

Most foods are harvested
from farms in the fall.

This machine is harvesting corn.

Potatoes

Potatoes are vegetables that grow under the ground. At harvest time, a *plow* turns the dirt to dig up the potatoes. Machines can dig four rows of potatoes at a time.

Potatoes

Corn

Corn is a vegetable that grows above the ground. When the silk on the corn turns gold or brown, the corn is ready to pick. Corn can grow so tall that people can hide in the rows.

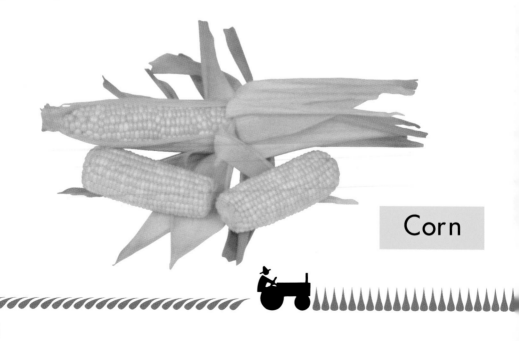

Corn

Silk

Pumpkins

Pumpkins are vegetables that grow on vines that grow across the top of the ground.

When the pumpkins are ready to harvest, they can be made into pies or jack-o'-lanterns!

Pumpkin

A pumpkin *patch*

Tomatoes

Tomatoes are fruits that grow on vines above the ground.

Ripe tomatoes are very soft. Most tomatoes are picked by hand so they won't get squashed.

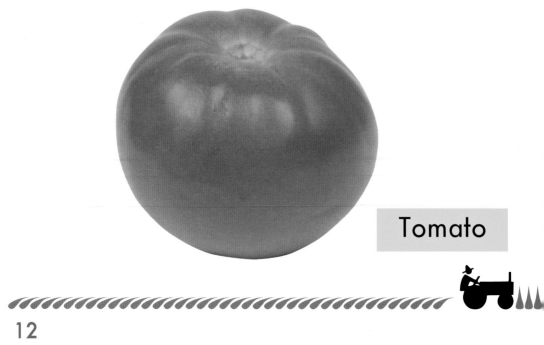

Tomato

Apples

Apples are fruits that grow on trees in an **orchard**.

Some people open
their apple orchards
to the public at harvest time
so people can pick
their own apples.

Apples

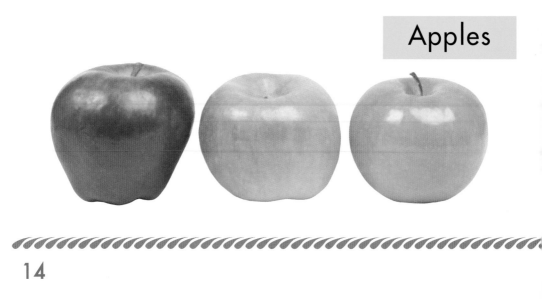

Cranberries

Cranberries are fruits that grow in a **bog**.

Cranberries that are used whole are scooped out with a rake.
Machines pick cranberries that are used in juices or sauces.

Cranberries

This machine is collecting floating cranberries.

To Market

Some fruits and vegetables go to packing plants, where they're packaged before going to grocery stores.

Some fruits and vegetables are sold at farmers' markets.

A farmers' market

Fun Facts

The biggest pumpkin ever grown weighed 1,061 pounds (482 kilograms). That's as much as a small car!

Aztecs grew the first tomatoes over 1,300 years ago in what is now Mexico.

Most potatoes grown in the United States are turned into french fries, potato chips, and other snack foods.

There are nearly 10,000 kinds of apples, but only a few kinds are sold in grocery stores.

Glossary

bog—an area of ground that is soft and wet

orchard—an area of land for growing fruit or nut trees

patch—a group of plants that are growing in one place

plow—a machine with a metal blade that breaks up and turns over dirt

Learn More

Books

Levenson, George. *Pumpkin Circle*. Berkeley, Calif.: Tricycle Press, 1999.

Rogers, Hal. *Combines*. Chanhassen, Minn.: The Child's World, 2001.

Royston, Angela. *Life Cycle of an Apple*. Des Plaines, Ill.: Heinemann Library, 1998.

Web Sites

Brain Pop

www.brainpop.com/science/seeall.weml (click on "autumn leaves")

Kidzone Fun Facts for Kids

www.kidzone.ws/plants/index.htm

Index

GR: G
Word Count: 228

From Jennifer Waters

I live near the Rocky Mountains.
The ocean is my favorite place.
I like to write songs and books.
I hope you enjoyed this book.